# Looking for Blackbeard's Treasure:
## Measuring the Distance

### by John Perritano

Content Consultant
David T. Hughes
*Mathematics Curriculum Specialist*

**N**ORWOOD**H**OUSE 🏠 **P**RESS
Chicago, IL

Norwood House Press
PO Box 316598
Chicago, IL 60631

For information regarding Norwood House Press, please visit our website at
www.norwoodhousepress.com or call 866-565-2900.

Special thanks to: Heidi Doyle
Production Management: Six Red Marbles
Editors: Linda Bullock and Kendra Muntz
Manufactured in North Mankato, Minnesota. 295R—062016

Paperback ISBN: 978-1-60357-500-3

The Library of Congress has cataloged the original hardcover edition with the following
call number: 2012027781

# CONTENTS

**Note to Caregivers:**

Throughout this book, many questions are posed to the reader. Some are open-ended and ask what the reader thinks. Discuss these questions with your child and guide him or her in thinking through the possible answers and outcomes. There are also questions posed which have a specific answer. Encourage your child to read through the text to determine the correct answer. Most importantly, encourage answers grounded in reality while also allowing imaginations to soar. Information to help support you as you share the book with your child is provided in the back in the **Additional Notes** section.

**Bold** words are defined in the glossary in the back of the book.

**15c**

Captain Edward Teach - *"Blackbeard"*

# BAHAMAS

4

# High Seas Adventure

*Ahoy, mateys!* Welcome aboard! Sit down and listen to a salty tale. It's a story of Edward Teach. *Ye* know him as Blackbeard the Pirate.

Blackbeard was the most feared pirate of his day. He was bloodthirsty. His beard was as black as coal. His eyes were like daggers.

He roamed the North Atlantic Ocean, looking for treasures like gold, silver, and jewels to steal. If *ye* got in his way, he'd blast *ye* ship to pieces. Even the most stouthearted men shook in their boots at the sight of Blackbeard's ship.

*Aye, what a ship it was!* Its name was *Queen Anne's Revenge*. Blackbeard got her as any good pirate would—he stole her.

Pirate ships sailed the seas looking for treasure to steal.

## Measuring Distance

For two long years, Blackbeard sailed. No place was safe from the *Queen Anne's Revenge.*

*Avast, ye scurvy dogs!* Blackbeard and his swashbucklers were sneaky. They tricked their victims, using the flags of their countries to sail close. When the ships were side-by-side, Blackbeard's men took the flag down. Then, they hoisted the skull and crossbones. *Arrrrrrrrrrggh!*

Like most pirate ships, *Queen Anne's Revenge* flew the skull and crossbones flag.

Most ships surrendered without a fight. Captains gave up their treasures. Other ship captains fought to the end. Their ships went to Davy Jones' Locker. That's pirate talk for the bottom of the ocean.

Blackbeard was crafty. He had many places to hide his treasure. To find some of Blackbeard's treasure, *ye* need to figure out the distance between each hiding place. How can *ye* do that?

**Idea 1:** You can use a ruler, a map, and a **map scale**. A map scale is the line on a map that explains distances on the map.

On the map below, 1 inch = 1 mile. So, if you measured 4 inches between two pirate hideouts, the real distance would be 4 miles.

1 inch = 1 mile

**Idea 2:** You can use a metric ruler, a meter stick, or a meter tape to measure distance in **metric units of length**. You can use a ruler, a yardstick, or a measuring tape to measure distances in **customary units of length**.

### Metric Units of Length

| millimeter (mm) |
| :---: |
| centimeter (cm) |
| meter (m) |
| kilometer (km) |

### Customary Units of Length

| inch (in.) |
| :---: |
| foot (ft.) |
| yard (yd.) |
| mile (mi.) |

**Idea 3:** You can change, or **convert**, units of length to make them easier to use. For example, you can change the smaller unit of inches into the larger unit of feet. Or you can convert the larger unit of kilometers into the smaller unit of meters. Using tables like these helps.

### Conversions of Customary Units of Length

| | |
|---|---|
| 12 inches | 1 foot |
| 24 inches | 2 feet |
| 36 inches | 3 feet |
| 3 feet | 1 yard |
| 1,760 yards | 1 mile |

### Conversions of Metric Units of Length

| | |
|---|---|
| 10 millimeters | 1 centimeter |
| 100 centimeters | 1 meter |
| 1,000 meters | 1 kilometer |

# DISCOVER ACTIVITY

**Materials**

- paper airplanes
- sponge balls
- plastic darts
- tape measure marked in customary or metric units
- paper and pencil

## Compare Distances

Find different objects that are easy to throw but don't go too far. Paper airplanes fly short distances. So do sponge balls and toy rubber darts.

Make a chart like this one. What unit will you measure with? Will it be feet or yards?

| Trial Number | Distance in Feet | Distance in Yards |
|:---:|:---:|:---:|
| Trial 1 | | |
| Trial 2 | | |
| Trial 3 | | |
| Trial 4 | | |
| Trial 5 | | |
| Trial 6 | | |
| Trial 7 | | |
| Trial 8 | | |

Now, throw the object you have chosen. Measure the distance it travels. Write the distance in your chart. Then, convert this distance into the other unit, and record it in the chart. Continue throwing and recording distances.

Now, record your distances on a **line plot**. A line plot lets you compare distances at a glance.

Draw a line. Label your line from 0 to the greatest distance in your chart. **Round** distances to the nearest whole number. For example, if a ball traveled $1\frac{1}{2}$ yards, round $1\frac{1}{2}$ to 2. Label the line with the units of measure that you used.

Then, make an X above each point on your line to show the distance the object traveled on each trial.

What distance occurs most often? Are any distances unusual? That is, are they outside most of the other distances?

Use this example of a line plot to understand how to build your own.

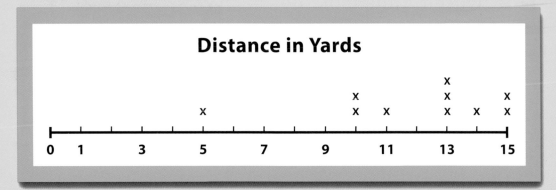

# The Queen's Pirate

There's more *ye* need to know about Blackbeard. Before becoming Blackbeard, Edward Teach was a young British seaman. He served on a privateer.

*Do ye know what a privateer is?* It's a privately owned ship. It's armed with cannons and guns. Governments hired privateers during wartime. They gave privateers permission to steal.

This is how Edward Teach made a name for himself. In 1701, the British went to war against France and Spain. In 1702, Queen Anne took the crown. She hired Teach to attack **enemy** ships. Teach was good at what he did. He forced many enemy ships to surrender their treasure.

 **What's the Word?**

Sailors use the word *broadside* to describe all of the weapons that fire from the side of a ship. They also use the word to describe when all of the guns fire at the same time.

Privateers like Teach did not want to destroy an enemy's ship. If a privateer sank a ship, the ship's treasure sank, too. So, a privateer's captain had to be clever. He had to sail his ship close enough to board the enemy's ship.

Imagine that the captain of a privateer made four attacks upon the enemy. He brought his ship these distances from enemy ships. How close did he get? Fill in the missing distances on this conversion table to find out.

| Attack | Distance | |
|:---:|:---:|:---:|
| 1 | 3 feet | 1 yard |
| 2 | 6 feet | ? |
| 3 | ? | 12 yards |
| 4 | 48 feet | ? |

Once the privateer was close, the captain was ready to attack. His crew jumped or climbed aboard the enemy ship and took its **booty** by force. Booty are goods taken by force.

How many feet closer did the captain get to the enemy in Attack 3 than in Attack 4?

# Pirates of the Caribbean

The war ended in 1714. Teach was out of work. So were other privateers. Some became pirates. They attacked ships from every nation, even England.

The Caribbean Islands became their home. The pirates captured the port of Nassau in the Bahamas. They chased away the city's honest citizens. In no time, Nassau became a lawless place. Teach made Nassau his home.

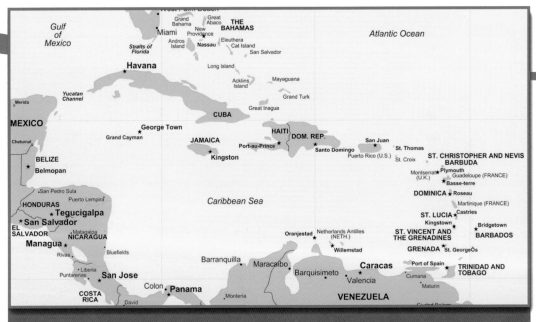

The Caribbean Sea is part of the Atlantic Ocean. Islands in the sea are called the Caribbean Islands. Although the Bahamas are not located in the sea, they are still part of the Caribbean community.

Teach and his sailors had once been British citizens. But now they were enemies of England. Teach took a different name. He became Blackbeard.

By 1718, the British had had enough of Teach and his fellow pirates. The British were willing to pardon the swashbucklers. That is, they agreed to forgive them of their crimes. The pirates would not go to prison if they stopped being pirates.

But Blackbeard didn't want a pardon. He wanted to be a pirate. He continued sailing the seas and stealing.

Look at the map scale below. Imagine that this scale was on a map Blackbeard used. He sailed 20 miles between ports. How many inches apart are the ports on a map?

If he sailed $2\frac{1}{2}$ miles between ports, how many inches apart are these ports on the map?

**One inch to five miles**

## Booty on a Line Plot

Blackbeard was king of the pirates. He grew a jet black beard. He carried three pistols. He hung pieces of rope from his hat. He then lit them on fire. *Shiver me timbers!* The smoke gave Blackbeard a devilish look. *Aye, mateys!* No one challenged Blackbeard.

Imagine that this line plot shows treasure Blackbeard stole. How many silver cups did Blackbeard steal? How many more daggers than swords did he steal? How many pieces of booty did he steal all together?

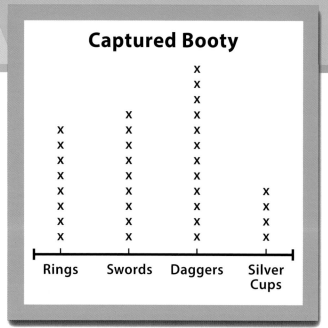

**Captured Booty**

```
                    x
                    x
                    x
            x       x
    x       x       x
    x       x       x
    x       x       x
    x       x       x
    x       x       x       x
    x       x       x       x
    x       x       x       x
    x       x       x       x
  ──────────────────────────────
   Rings  Swords  Daggers  Silver
                            Cups
```

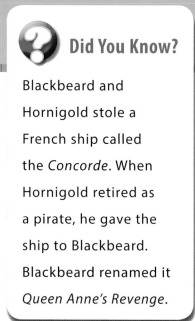

**Did You Know?**

Blackbeard and Hornigold stole a French ship called the *Concorde*. When Hornigold retired as a pirate, he gave the ship to Blackbeard. Blackbeard renamed it *Queen Anne's Revenge*.

## Ransom

Blackbeard once captured a large cargo ship. The ship had sailed out of Charleston Harbor in South Carolina. Many wealthy passengers were onboard. Some were children, as old as *ye*.

Blackbeard locked everyone below the deck. It was dark. It was musty. The pirate threatened to kill everyone if the townspeople in Charleston did not pay a **ransom**. The children were scared. Mothers cried. What did Blackbeard want? A chest filled with medicine.

The deadline passed. The **hostages** waited to die. With only seconds left, the chest arrived. Blackbeard let his hostages go. He stole their jewelry before they left.

Imagine Blackbeard buried the jewelry he stole. The red X on the map shows where he hid it. The scale on the map is $\frac{1}{2}$ inch: 5 miles. The distance between the red X and the port where Blackbeard landed is three inches. What distance is it?

# Connecting to Art

*Ahoy!* Who loves a pirate? Many people do, especially those who go to the movies.

"Captain Blood" was a famous pirate movie made in 1935. Errol Flynn played a doctor who becomes a pirate. He took from the rich and gave to the poor.

In 1953, Peter Pan faced the pirate Captain Hook. Captain Hook commanded a ship called the *Jolly Roger*. His crew sang "A Pirate's Life for Me."

Captain Jack Sparrow appeared in a series of movies called "Pirates of the Caribbean." Sparrow was a pirate with a heart. He called his ship the *Black Pearl*.

# Meters from Tortuga

Hideouts were important. Pirates had many in the Caribbean and along the American coast.

New Providence in the Bahamas was a safe port. The city had a shallow **harbor**. The water wasn't deep enough for British warships to sail close.

Another famous pirate hideout was an island shaped like a turtle. It was named Tortuga, the Spanish word for "turtle." Tortuga belongs to Haiti.

French, English, and Dutch pirates lived on the island. They sailed from the island's only harbor and returned home with treasures.

Find Tortuga on the old map shown here. A band of water 12 km wide separates the island from the main island of Haiti. How many meters wide is that band of water? Remember: 1 km = 1,000 m.

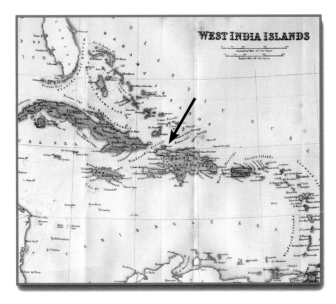

Port Royal was another pirate hideout. It was in Jamaica. The harbor was easy to guard. And it was deep. Ships could load and unload easily.

The port city grew in size and importance. Traders grew rich. Pirates grew rich, too. They raided cities from nearby South America and brought their treasures back to Port Royal.

Imagine a pirate captain returns to Port Royal with stolen treasure. Among the treasure is a chest of Spanish coins.

The wooden chest is $2\frac{1}{2}$ yards long. How many feet long is it?

The chest is $\frac{1}{2}$ yard wide. How many feet wide is it?

The chest is one yard tall. How many feet tall is it?

# Good Neighbor

Blackbeard was bad. Yet, North Carolina's governor gave Blackbeard a safe place to live. At the time, North Carolina was a British **colony**. The governor gave Blackbeard one of several islands off the North Carolina coast. From these islands, Blackbeard could attack ships sailing up the coast.

People living on the islands did not mind having Blackbeard as a neighbor. They bought the goods he stole for very little money.

Make believe this line plot shows the goods Blackbeard sold. How many more barrels of flour did Blackbeard sell than wheels of cheese? After flour, what other item did Blackbeard sell the most of? How many barrels, wheels, and bolts did Blackbeard steal all together?

# Death of a Ship

By 1718, Blackbeard had four ships and about 300 sailors. A year earlier, Blackbeard had met the pirate Stede Bonnet. Bonnet had money and a ship, but he knew little about running a pirate crew. He agreed to give Blackbeard control of his ship, *Revenge*. Blackbeard played a trick on Bonnet. He wanted to get more stolen **loot** for himself. So, he ran his ships the *Queen Anne's Revenge* and *Adventure* **aground**.

He convinced Bonnet to leave *Revenge* with him, while Bonnet went to seek a pardon from England's king.

After Bonnet left, Blackbeard got *Adventure* afloat again. Then, he took the treasure from his ships and the *Revenge* and sailed away.

In 1996, scientists found the wreck of *Queen Anne's Revenge* off the coast of North Carolina. It was covered with 20 feet of water. Scientists found a bronze bell and 21 cannons.

Imagine you see a map of the seafloor around the wreck. On the map, the distance between a cannon and the bell is three inches. The scale on this map is 1 inch = 50 feet. How far apart are the two objects?

Alexander Spotswood was the governor of Virginia in 1718. He heard that Blackbeard was on his favorite island off the coast. Blackbeard held a huge party for pirates far and wide. Spotswood took this as his chance to get rid of Blackbeard forever.

The governor sent two British ships to the island. The ships were led by Robert Maynard.

When Blackbeard saw the ships coming, he knew he was trapped. Only **sandbars** near the island could protect him. The British waited for the morning tide so they could sail over the sandbars.

This new ship is a model of a pirate ship like those that sailed in Blackbeard's time.

As they waited, the British prepared for battle. So did Blackbeard and his pirates. The pirates got their cannons ready to fire. They poured water over blankets to put out fires. They put sand on the deck to soak up any blood that might be spilled during the upcoming battle.

"*If ye die on the morrow, does your wife, Mary, know where ye buried the treasure?*" one pirate asked Blackbeard.

Blackbeard laughed. "*My friend,*" he said, "*nobody but me and the Devil knows where it's hid.*"

Morning came. Blackbeard did not try to run away. He waited at the wheel of his ship. Maynard moved in for the kill. Blackbeard then set sail.

He steered the ship toward the beach near a small sandbar. Maynard's ships followed. Both crashed into the sandbar. The pirates opened fire. They blasted one navy ship to bits. Then, Blackbeard's ship hit a sandbar, too.

Blackbeard's cannons fired. Fill in the missing distances on this table to find out how far the cannonballs traveled. Remember 1 yd = 3 ft.

| Cannon | Yards | Feet |
|--------|-------|------|
| 1 | 450 | ? |
| 2 | 325 | ? |
| 3 | 290 | ? |
| 4 | 410 | ? |

Maynard had to move his ship from the sandbar, or die. He ordered his men to throw the ship's stores of food and water overboard. The ship became lighter and broke free. It edged toward Blackbeard's ship. As it did, Maynard's men hid below decks. Blackbeard's men didn't see anyone on deck. They thought the British ship was empty.

When they were close, Maynard's men jumped out and boarded the pirate ship. The British fired their pistols. They slashed with their swords.

Screams filled the air. Finally, Blackbeard faced Maynard. Each fired their pistols. Blackbeard missed, but Maynard didn't. Wounded, Blackbeard raised his sword to strike Maynard. Just then, a British seaman shot Blackbeard from behind and killed him.

# Math at Work

In Blackbeard's time, **navigators** steered their ships. They used two tools to know where they were going, a **compass** and a **quadrant**.

A quadrant has a straight edge and a curved edge. Navigators often hung the quadrant in the sails or put it on a stand to keep it steady.

They pointed the straight edge to the sun during the day and the North Star at night. Then, they measured the angle between the star and the horizon. This gave them a **latitude**, or horizontal line of measurement. They then used the compass to travel east or west along the line of latitude.

The small ball hanging from the quadrant is called a plumb bob. When the plumb bob is still, the quadrant is level.

*Aye, landlubbers, this ends our salty tale.* Or does it? No one has ever found Blackbeard's treasure. The secret died with him. As I tell *ye* this story, people still look.

Some say the crafty Blackbeard buried a treasure chest at the foot of a tree on Ocracoke Island in 1717. Others say he dumped it in a river near one of his other hideouts. It's possible. Blackbeard had several hideouts in North Carolina.

Imagine that you find a map like the one on this page that will take you to Blackbeard's treasure. You are where the ship is marked on the map. You use a ruler to measure the distance between you and the treasure on the map.

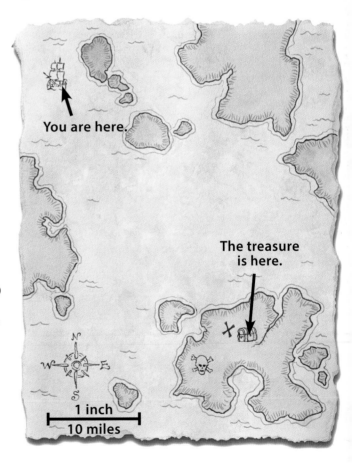

You are here.

The treasure is here.

1 inch
10 miles

The distance you measure on the map is 3 inches. How will you figure out how far you must go to find the treasure?

**Idea 1:** The map has a **map scale**. Use the map scale to figure out how far away you are from the treasure.

**Idea 2:** Measure in Metric or Customary **Units of length**. What units of length does the scale use? In this case, the units are inches. They are customary units of length.

**Idea 3: Convert** units. Will converting measurements help you understand the distance more easily? The units are in inches. Converting them to another unit won't be helpful.

How far away is the treasure?

*Off ye go, ye swashbuckling treasure hunters. May the wind be at your back and the sea below your feet. And remember, yo, ho, ho....*

# WHAT COMES NEXT?

## Make a Treasure Map

Think about a space where you often play. It may be in your back yard. It may be in a neighborhood park.

Plan a treasure hunt for your friends. Make the map look old, like a forgotten pirate's map.

Follow these steps:

- Fill a box with whatever treasure you choose.
- Hide the treasure. You don't have to bury it. You can hide it among or behind objects.
- Tear the edges of some thick white paper to make it look old.
- Draw your treasure map. Mark the map with the letter X to show where the treasure is. Include objects on your map, such as trees or play equipment.
- Measure distances between objects. Put a scale on your map.
- Pour tea into a shallow pan. Wet the paper in the tea. Remove the paper, crumple it, and leave it to dry.
- Unfold the map. Give it to your friends. Let the fun begin.

# GLOSSARY

**aground:** on land.

**booty:** stolen goods worth money, such as gold and jewels.

**colony:** one of the early British settlements in North America.

**compass:** a tool for telling direction.

**convert:** to change units of one measuring system to units of another.

**customary units of length:** Inches, feet, yards, and miles are customary units of length.

**enemy:** an opponent, especially during wartime.

**harbor:** a port on a body of water and near a coast in which ships can anchor safely.

**hostages:** people held against their will.

**latitude:** a distance north or south of the equator.

**line plot:** a diagram that shows the number of times data occur.

**loot:** goods taken by force.

**map scale:** a comparison of distance on a map and the same distance in the real world. For example, 1 inch = 10 miles; 3 centimeters = 2.5 kilometers.

**metric units of length:** Millimeters, centimeters, meters, and kilometers are metric units of length.

**navigators:** people who steer a ship or other vehicle.

**quadrant:** a tool sailors used to determine their location while at sea.

**ransom:** a sum of money demanded or paid for the release of a prisoner.

**round:** to find the nearest whole number.

**sandbars:** ridges of sand that are hidden beneath water.

# FURTHER READING

FICTION

*Blackbeard's Last Fight,* by Eric A. Kimmel, Farrar, Straus and Giroux, 2006

NONFICTION

*Blackbeard the Pirate King,* by J. Patrick Lewis, National Geographic Children's Books, 2006

*Measurement: The Measured Mystery,* by Emily Sohn and Katie Sharp, Norwood House Press, 2011

# ADDITIONAL NOTES

**The page references below provide answers to questions asked throughout the book. Questions whose answers will vary are not addressed.**

**Page 13:** 6 feet = 2 yards

36 feet = 12 yards

48 feet = 16 yards;
The captain got 12 feet closer.

**Page 15:** 20 miles = 4 inches
$2\frac{1}{2}$ miles = $\frac{1}{2}$ inch

**Page 16:** 4 silver cups. He stole 3 more daggers than swords. He stole 33 pieces of booty all together.

**Page 17:** 30 miles

**Page 19:** 12,000 meters

**Page 20:** $7\frac{1}{2}$ feet long; $1\frac{1}{2}$ feet wide; 3 feet tall

**Page 21:** 2 more barrels of flour; nails. Blackbeard stole 14 barrels, wheels, and bolts all together.

**Page 22:** 150 feet apart

**Page 24:** 1,350 feet; 975 feet; 870 feet; 1,230 feet

**Page 28:** 30 miles

# INDEX

# CONTENT CONSULTANT

**David T. Hughes**

David is an experienced mathematics teacher, writer, presenter, and adviser. He serves as a consultant for the Partnership for Assessment of Readiness for College and Careers. David has also worked as the Senior Program Coordinator for the Charles A. Dana Center at The University of Texas at Austin and was an editor and contributor for the *Mathematics Standards in the Classroom* series.